ANTHOLOGISE

The Poetry of Earth is Never Dead

ANTHOLOGISE
The Poetry of Earth is Never Dead

An Anthology of Ecology Poetry by Monkton Senior School

PICADOR

First published 2013 by Picador
an imprint of Pan Macmillan, a division of Macmillan Publishers Limited
Pan Macmillan, 20 New Wharf Road, London N1 9RR
Basingstoke and Oxford
Associated companies throughout the world
www.panmacmillan.com

ISBN 978-1-4472-2179-1

Selection and arrangement copyright © Monkton Senior School 2013
Illustrations copyright © the individual illustrators 2013
Foreword copyright © Carol Ann Duffy 2013
Foreword copyright © HRH The Duchess of Cornwall 2013
The permissions acknowledgements on pp. 77–78 constitute an extension of this copyright page.

The right of Monkton Senior School to be identified as the
editors of this work has been asserted by them in accordance
with the Copyright, Designs and Patents Act 1988.

All rights reserved. No part of this publication may be
reproduced, stored in or introduced into a retrieval system, or
transmitted, in any form, or by any means (electronic, mechanical,
photocopying, recording or otherwise) without the prior written
permission of the publisher. Any person who does any unauthorized
act in relation to this publication may be liable to criminal
prosecution and civil claims for damages.

The Macmillan Group has no responsibility for the information provided by
any author websites whose address you obtain from this book ('author websites').
The inclusion of author website addresses in this book does not constitute
an endorsement by or association with us of such sites or the content,
products, advertising or other materials presented on such sites.

9 8 7 6 5 4 3 2 1

A CIP catalogue record for this book is available from
the British Library.

Printed and bound by CPI Group (UK) Ltd, Croydon, CR0 4YY

This book is sold subject to the condition that it shall not,
by way of trade or otherwise, be lent, re-sold, hired out,
or otherwise circulated without the publisher's prior consent
in any form of binding or cover other than that in which
it is published and without a similar condition including this
condition being imposed on the subsequent purchaser.

Visit **www.picador.com** to read more about all our books
and to buy them. You will also find features, author interviews and
news of any author events, and you can sign up for e-newsletters
so that you're always first to hear about our new releases.

Foreword by Carol Ann Duffy

I'd like to begin this foreword by thanking all the schools, teachers and students combined, who entered the Anthologise competition and participated so whole-heartedly in this project designed to get young people reading and discussing poetry in a new way. I also thank Helen Taylor, Morag Styles, John Agard, Grace Nichols, Gillian Clarke, Kaye Tewe and James Draper from the Writing School at Manchester Metropolitan University, the Poetry Book Society, the Bath Literature Festival, Picador, Waterstones and HRH The Duchess of Cornwall. Most importantly, I warmly congratulate the winners of Anthologise, Monkton Senior School, for their quite superb *The Poetry of Earth is Never Dead*. Unless we have English teachers who are passionate about literature we cannot have good young readers of poetry, and Anthologise was designed to encourage students to closely read poetry, from Anon onwards, and to edit their own new anthologies through critical group discussion. The successful young editors here demonstrate to us all that you can select a theme and say something classy, fresh and surprising through the choice and juxtaposition of poems, and in *The Poetry of Earth is Never Dead* we have a big theme for our time. The poems here speak to each other and, I am sure, will capture a whole new audience of young people as well as those of us who regularly read poetry. The selection also reveals very impressive research which encompasses single collections and pamphlets – quite amazing considering our schools are very often short of the budgets to buy these, relying more often than not on anthologies. But here is a school which has produced its own fantastic anthology, using all of its resources, not least human, and has gifted us a wonderful variety of poetry in terms of form, theme and language, with moving and often startling choices. It is an anthology with a voice which I hope will encourage all schools to take up the thrilling challenge of engaging with poetry in this way and to produce their own anthologies.

ANTHOLOGISE

The Poetry of Earth is Never Dead

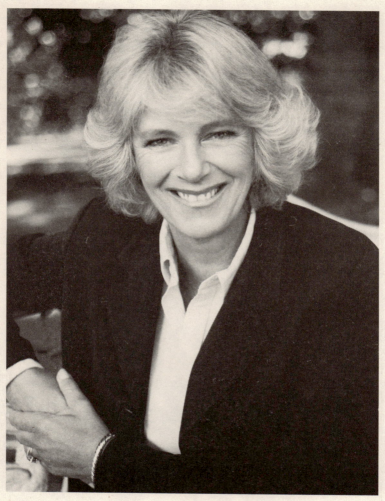
Photograph © Mario Testino

I am delighted to lend my support to this truly inspirational competition, *Anthologise*, run by the Poet Laureate and to introduce readers to this most sparkling and topical winner.

In reaching out to so many of our schools, to both students and teachers, *Anthologise* demonstrates the importance not only of reading, but of sharing and discussing the substance, relevance and beauty of our reading and our poetry. It has been an immense joy to see the enthusiasm of so many young people who participated nationally in this project and I heartily congratulate the winners on this wonderful winning entry *The Poetry of Earth is Never Dead*.

Camilla

Contents

Foreword by Monkton Senior School　　　　　　　　　　　xv

APPRECIATION OF NATURE

On the Grasshopper and Cricket John Keats	3
Through That Door John Cotton	4
My Idle Dreams Roam Far Li Yu	6
The Praise of Spring Gonzalo de Berceo	7
Earth Songs John Clarke	9
The Earth and the People Inuit	11
'Loveliest of trees, the cherry now' A. E. Housman	12
Sonnet John Clare	13
The Negro Speaks of Rivers Langston Hughes	14
earth cries Jean 'Binta' Breeze	15
Moss-Gathering Theodore Roethke	16

CYCLE OF NATURE

An Alphabet for the Planet Riad Nourallah	19
Death of a Naturalist Seamus Heaney	21
Place W. S. Merwin	23
The River in March Ted Hughes	24
A Beetle Called Derek Benjamin Zephaniah	26
Nature Loriah Leah	28

HUMAN ECOLOGY

Cultivators	Susan Taylor	31
The Shepherd	William Blake	32
The Case	Kathleen Jamie	33
The Magnificent Bull	*Dinka tribe*	34
Close to Nature	Nnamdi Ben Nneji	35
Inside my Zulu Hut	Oswald Mbuyiseni Mtshali	37
I Tell the Bees	Jo Shapcott	38
Gathering the Honey	Virgil	39

DESTRUCTION

Nothing Gold can Stay	Robert Frost	43
'Report to Wordsworth'	Boey Kim Cheng	44
Lily of the Valley	Alice Oswald	45
Trailing Arbutus	Gloria Sarasin	46
Endangered Species	David Constantine	48
The Flower-Fed Buffaloes	Vachel Lindsay	50
Pheasant	Sylvia Plath	51
Almanac	Primo Levi	53
Estuary	Ian Hamilton Finlay	54
Harvest Hymn	John Betjeman	55
The Recital of Lost Cities	Lavinia Greenlaw	56
The Woman in the Moon	Carol Ann Duffy	58

BEGIN AFRESH FRESH AFRESH 59

The Trees Philip Larkin — 61
The Eclipse Richard Eberhart — 62
The Cloud (excerpts from . . .) Percy Bysshe Shelley — 63
Si Dieu N'existait Pas John Burnside — 65
Heavenly Grass Tennessee Williams — 66
Untitled – (Tomorrow's Child) Glenn Thomas — 67
I'm Alive, I Believe In Everything Lesley Choyce — 68
A Light Exists in Spring Emily Dickinson — 70

Monkton School and the Anthologise Competition — 73
Acknowledgements — 75
Permission acknowledgements — 76

Foreword by Monkton Senior School

Monkton Senior School's commitment to the environment, working towards Green Flag status, helped make the pupil s' choice of theme for their anthology simple; reflecting the school's desire for a sustainable future.

The pupils were inspired to search for poetry which meant something to them and each member of the group was tasked with justifying their first choice for inclusion; here are just a few of their thoughts.

Daniel Mangles (aged fourteen) chose 'Through that Door' by John Cotton. 'The first thing that strikes me in this poem is the breathtaking montage which I experience through the door. This is no rigid, predetermined version; it brings to mind all things I regard as beautiful, fluidly following each other past this view for me to see. The beauty of this poem is the way in which the descriptions are so vague yet so appealing . . .'

Sian Cogan (aged fourteen) chose 'Close to Nature' by Nmadi Ben Nneji. 'This poem creates a vivid image of what nature is like in its most simple form . . .very often I feel ecology is seen as about animals and their environment, but it is forgotten that we also come under that category – we forget the enormous impact on ourselves . . .'

Robert Warwood-Hart (aged thirteen) chose 'A Beetle Called Derek' by Benjamin Zephaniah. 'This poem speaks out to me because of its viewpoint. I think it is made brilliant because of its simplicity – making the poem innocent, which in my opinion makes it affect you more . . .'

Holly Phoa (aged fifteen) chose 'Lily of the Valley' by Alice Oswald. 'It was me. I picked this poem. I picked it because it spoke to me. So many images rushed to my head. I was inspired by the ideas that sparked in my already over-active imagination. As a lover of art, as a lover of telling stories with pictures, I was bombarded by the possibilities of how I could create a picture to tell this story. I love to be inspired and I picked this poem so that it can inspire you.'

Sarah Pritchard (aged seventeen) chose 'Tomorrow's Child' by Glenn Thomas. 'What I loved about this poem was that it is written almost in the style of a letter, as if the poet is talking directly to "tomorrow's child", whom I too felt I had not really met until this reading. It is difficult to imagine what the world will be like in twenty or so years' time. Looking after the environment can often seem like a lost cause, but when I read this poem I realize that the next generation (and potentially my children) will face the same environmental issues as we do now.'

The joy of assembling this anthology has enabled the Library to work closely with the Art Department. This has been a great success and challenge for all concerned.

APPRECIATION OF NATURE

AND THE RIVERS AND THE FOREST OF THE GREAT OUTDOORS

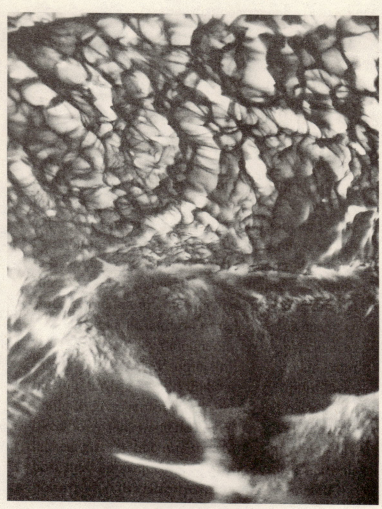
Illustration by Sarah Pritchard year 13

On the Grasshopper and Cricket

The poetry of earth is never dead:
    When all the birds are faint with the hot sun,
    And hide in cooling trees, a voice will run
From hedge to hedge about the new-mown mead –
That is the Grasshopper's. He takes the lead
    In summer luxury; he has never done
    With his delights, for when tired out with fun
He rests at ease beneath some pleasant weed.
The poetry of earth is ceasing never:
    On a lone winter evening, when the frost
    Has wrought a silence, from the stove there shrills
The Cricket's song, in warmth increasing ever,
    And seems to one in drowsiness half lost,
    The Grasshopper's among some grassy hills.

                                  John Keats

Through That Door

Through that door
Is a garden with a wall,
The red brick crumbling,
The lupins growing tall,
Where the lawn is like a carpet
Spread for you,
And it's all as tranquil
As you never knew.

Through that door
Is the great ocean-sea
Which heaves and rolls
To eternity,
With its islands and promontories
Waiting for you
To explore and discover
In that vastness of blue.

Through that door
Is your secret room
Where the window lets in
The light of the moon,
With its mysteries and magic
Where you can find
Thrills and excitements
Of every kind.

Through that door
Are the mountains and the moors
And the rivers and the forests
Of the great outdoors,
All the plains and the ice-caps
And lakes as blue as sky
For all those creatures
That walk or swim or fly.

Through that door
Is a city of the mind
Where you can imagine
What you'll find
You can make of that city
What you want it to,
And if you choose to share it,
Then it could come true.

                John Cotton

My Idle Dreams Roam Far

My idle dreams roam far,
　　To the southern land where spring is fragrant.
　　Wind and strings play on a boat on the river's clear surface,
　　The city is full of catkins flying like light dust.
　　People are occupied admiring the flowers.
My idle dreams roam far,
　　To the southern land where autumn is clear.
　　For a thousand li over rivers and hills cold colours stretch far,
　　Deep in flowering reeds, a solitary boat is moored.
　　Beneath the bright moon, a flute plays in the tower.

　　　　　　　　　　　　　　　　　　Li Yu (Chinese)

(li — traditional Chinese measure of distance, today standardised at 500 metres.)

The Praise of Spring

I, Gonzalo de Berceo, in the gentle summertide,
Wending upon a pilgrimage, came to a meadow's side;
All green was it and beautiful, with flowers far and wide, –
A pleasant spot, I ween, wherein the traveller might abide.

Flowers with the sweetest odors filled all the sunny air,
And not alone refreshed the sense, but stole the mind from every care;
On every side a fountain gushed, whose waters pure and fair,
Ice-cold beneath the summer sun, but warm in winter were.

There on the thick and shadowy trees, amid the foliage green,
Were the fig and the pomegranate, the pear and apple seen;
And other fruits of various kinds, the tufted leaves between,
None were unpleasant to the taste and none decayed, I ween.

The verdure of the meadow green, the odor of the flowers,
The grateful shadows of the trees, tempered with fragrant showers,
Refreshed me in the burning heat of the sultry noontide hours;
Oh, one might live upon the balm and fragrance of those bowers!

Ne'er had I found on earth a spot that had such power to please,
Such shadows from the summer sun, such odors on the breeze;
I threw my mantle on the ground, that I might rest at ease,
And stretched upon the greensward lay in the shadow of the trees.

There soft reclining in the shade, all cares beside me flung,
I heard the soft and mellow notes that through the woodland rung;
Ear never listened to a strain, for instrument or tongue,
So mellow and harmonious as the songs above me sung.

> Gonzalo de Berceo (1180–1246)
> From *The Miracles of our Lady* by Gonzalo de Berceo,
> translated by H. W. Longfellow

Earth Songs

Hear it in whisper
Morning mist
Drifting skeins of wool
Rising from water.

Hear it in squeaks, cries
Blather, jabber, prattle
Tumbling over each other
Chicks need feeding squawks.

Hear it in rumble, grumble
Pebbles pulled dragged
Wave after wave
Shuffle or shingle.

Hear it in madflap
Canvas in a gale
Angry wingbeats of heron
Rising from reeds.

Hear it in wind
Racing around tree tops
Blasting over fields
Bawling in your face.

Hear it in thunder
Bellowing around the valley.
Hear it in storming rain
Clamouring, howling . . .

Hear it in the mountains
The sea and the sky:
I am the earth
The earth
The earth.

        John Clarke

The Earth and the People

The earth was here before the people.
    The very first people
    came out of the ground.
Everything came from the ground,
    even caribou.
Children once grew
    out of the ground
    just as flowers do.
Women out wandering
    found them sprawling on the grass
    and took them home and nursed them.
That way people multiplied.

This land of ours
    has become habitable
    because we came here
And learned how to hunt.

Inuit

'Loveliest of trees, the cherry now'
(from *A Shropshire Lad*)

Loveliest of trees, the cherry now
Is hung with bloom along the bough,
And stands about the woodland ride
Wearing white for Eastertide.

Now, of my threescore years and ten,
Twenty will not come again,
And take from seventy springs a score,
It only leaves me fifty more.

And since to look at things in bloom
Fifty springs are little room,
About the woodlands I will go
To see the cherry hung with snow.

A. E. Housman

Sonnet

I love to see the summer beaming forth
And white wool sack clouds sailing to the north
I love to see the wild flowers come again
And mare blobs stain with gold the meadow drain
And water lillies whiten on the floods
Where reed clumps rustle like a wind shook wood
Where from her hiding place the moor hen pushes
And seeks her flag nest floating in bull rushes
I like the willow leaning half way o'er
The clear deep lake to stand upon its shore
I love the hay grass when the flower head swings
To summer winds and insects' happy wings
That sport about the meadow the bright day
And see bright beetles in the clear lake play

John Clare

The Negro Speaks of Rivers

I've known rivers:
I've known rivers ancient as the world and older than the
    flow of human blood in human veins.

My soul has grown deep like the rivers.

I bathed in the Euphrates when dawns were young.
I built my hut near the Congo and it lulled me to sleep.
I looked upon the Nile and raised the pyramids above it.
I heard the singing of the Mississippi when Abe Lincoln
    went down to New Orleans, and I've seen its muddy
    bosom turn all golden in the sunset.

I've known rivers:
Ancient, dusky rivers.

My soul has grown deep like the rivers.

                                            Langston Hughes

earth cries

she doesn't cry for water
she runs rivers very deep
she doesn't cry for food
she has suckled trees
she doesn't cry for clothing
she weaves all that she wears
she doesn't cry for shelter
she grows thatch everywhere
she doesn't cry for children
she's got more than she can bear
she doesn't cry for heaven
she knows it's always there
you don't know why she's crying
when she's got everything
how could you know she's crying
for just one humane being

                Jean 'Binta' Breeze

Moss-Gathering

To loosen with all ten fingers held wide and limber
And lift up a patch, dark-green, the kind for lining cemetery baskets,
Thick and cushiony, like an old-fashioned doormat,
The crumbling small hollow sticks on the underside mixed with roots,
And wintergreen berries and leaves still stuck to the top, –
That was moss-gathering.
But something always went out of me when I dug loose the carpets
Of green, or plunged to my elbows in the spongy yellowish moss of
   the marshes:
And afterwards I always felt mean, jogging back over the logging road,
As if I had broken the natural order of things in that swampland;
Disturbed some rhythm, old and of vast importance,
By pulling off flesh from the living planet;
As if I had committed, against the whole scheme of life, a desecration.

                                        Theodore Roethke

CYCLE OF NATURE

COLOUR OF LIFE WE'LL HELP TO SPREAD

Illustration by Zi Wu year 13

An Alphabet for the Planet

A for air.
The gentle breeze by which we live.
B for bread.
A food to bake and take – and *give*.
C for climate.
It can be warm, it can be cold . . .
D for dolphin.
A smiling friend no net should hold.
E for earth.
Our ship through space, and home to share.
F for family,
Which also means people *everywhere*.
G for green.
Colour of life we'll help to spread.
H for healthy.
Happy and strong, no fumes with lead.
I for ivory.
The elephant's tusks, his own to keep.
J for jungle.
A rainforest. No axe should creep.
K for kindly.
To everyone, gentle and good.
L for Life.
It fills the sea and town and wood.
M for mother.
She may feel hurt, but loves us all.
N for nest.

A tiny home for chicks so small.
O for ozone.
It shields our Earth from harmful rays.
P for peace.
'My happy dream,' the Planet says.
Q for quiet.
Where no loud noise can get at you.
R for recycled.
Old cans and cards as good as new.
S for Sun.
The nearest star. It gives us light.
T for tree,
A grander plant, a green delight.
U for united.
Working as one to put things right.
V for victory.
Winning over disease and war.
W for water.
The whole earth drinks when rainclouds pour.
X for Xylophone.
Music from wood – the high notes soar!
Y for yummy.
Those tasty fruits 'organically grown'.
Z for zoo.
A cage a condor – sad, alone.

                              Riad Nourallah

Death of a Naturalist

All year the flax-dam festered in the heart
Of the townland; green and heavy headed
Flax had rotted there, weighted down by huge sods.
Daily it sweltered in the punishing sun.
Bubbles gargled delicately, bluebottles
Wove a strong gauze of sound around the smell.
There were dragon-flies, spotted butterflies,
But best of all was the warm thick slobber
Of frogspawn that grew like clotted water
In the shade of the banks. Here, every spring
I would fill jampotfulls of the jellied
Specks to range on window-sills at home,
On shelves at school, and wait and watch until
The fattening dots burst into nimble-
Swimmimg tadpoles. Miss Walls would tell us how
The daddy frog was called a bullfrog
And how he croaked and how the mammy frog
Laid hundreds of eggs and this was frogspawn.
You could tell the weather by frogs too
For they were yellow in the sun and brown
In rain.

   Then one hot day when fields were rank
With cowdung in the grass the angry frogs
Invaded the flax-dam; I ducked through hedges
To a coarse croaking that I had not heard
Before. The air was thick with a bass chorus.

Right down the dam gross-bellied frogs were cocked
On sods; their loose necks pulsed like sails. Some hopped:
The slap and plop were obscene threats. Some sat
Poised like mud grenades, their blunt heads farting.
I sickened, turned and ran. The great slime kings
Were gathered there for vengeance and I knew
That if I dipped my hand the spawn would clutch it.

                                          Seamus Heaney

Place

On the last day of the world
I would want to plant a tree

what for
not for the fruit

the tree that bears the fruit
is not the one that was planted

I want the tree that stands in
the earth for the first time

with the sun
already going down

and the water
touching its roots

in the earth full of the dead
and the clouds passing

one by one
over its leaves

                W. S. Merwin

The River in March

Now the river is rich, but her voice is low.
It is her Mighty Majesty the sea
Travelling among the villages incognito.

Now the river is poor. No song, just a thin mad whisper.
The winter floods have ruined her.
She squats between draggled banks, fingering her rags and rubbish.

And now the river is rich. A deep choir.
It is the lofty clouds, that work in heaven,
Going on their holiday to the sea.

The river is poor again. All her bones are showing.
Through a dry wig of bleached flotsam she peers up ashamed
From her slum of sticks.

Now the river is rich, collecting shawls and minerals.
Rain brought fatness, but she takes ninety-nine percent
Leaving the fields just one percent to survive on.

And now she is poor. Now she is East wind sick.
She huddles in holes and corners. The brassy sun gives her a headache.
She has lost all her fish. And she shivers.

But now once more she is rich. She is viewing her lands.
A hoard of king-cups spills from her folds, it blazes, it cannot be hidden.
A salmon, a sow of solid silver,

Bulges to glimpse it.

                                                    Ted Hughes

A Beetle Called Derek

There once was a Beetle called Derek
Who lived in a forest on Earth
And this little Beetle called Derek
Was really attracted to dirt,
She did not carry no weapons
Except what she naturally got
She did not have no possessions
But she could look after her lot.

The forest protected our Derek
Predators came and they went,
This was no reason to panic
Cause this was with Nature's consent,
She was related to Wind and Fire
A sister of necessity,
She was related to Earth and Water
A distant cousin to me.
Doctors could not work out Derek
Derek had secrets she kept,
Then came the white coated bandits
Scientists seeking all they could get,
Her home was robbed to make paper
And that got the climate upset,
Cows would graze to make burgers
The cows never made a profit!!

Derek was taken for granted
By selfish, non-beetle people,
Some supporters of Derek demanded
An end to what we call Evil,
Handouts could not solve the problem alone
So I called out the Eco-Police,
But we could not win the fight on our own
Now Derek my friend is deceased.

There once was a beetle called Derek
Who lived in a forest on Earth,
Nobody knew where she came from
A kind of mysterious birth,
I built a memorial to Derek
Hoping that it may be seen,
I hope when I die I'll see Derek,
In a heaven organic and green.

     Benjamin Zephaniah

Nature

spider spinning slowly
birds blissfully chirping softly
deer cuddled with fawn

        Loriah Leah

HUMAN ECOLOGY

WE WHO WORK WITH EARTH AND STEEL

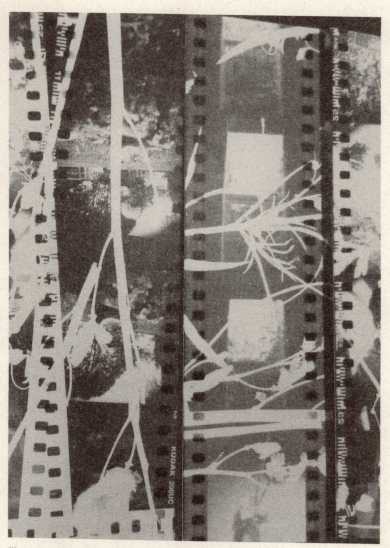
Illustration by Christina Lee year 13

Cultivators

   We,
who work with earth and steel
and feel winter frozen in our hands
where fields are looms,
weave the patterns of crops;
damp loam flows like silk
through shuttling metal.

   And our hills,
with their wild uncurbable wills
may be hard to till
but are easy to love,
steep work weakens the tractor
but strengthens the heart.

                    Susan Taylor

The Shepherd
(from *Songs of Innocence*)

How sweet is the shepherd's sweet lot!
From the morn to the evening he strays;
He shall follow his sheep all the day,
And his tongue shall be filled with praise.

For he hears the lambs' innocent call,
And he hears the ewes' tender reply;
He is watchful while they are in peace,
For they know when their shepherd is nigh.

William Blake

The Case

In which river did the fish swim
that mistook for a fly a hook on a line
so drew its last, that a silver blade
could pare from its flesh its still fresh
weed-green skin, to be cured
then eased around this little case,
which contains the doctor's
shoal of fleams, and the keen one
he's pressing now to your inner arm,
so a mere flick opens a vein

      Kathleen Jamie

Illustration by Nicola Murray year 13

The Magnificent Bull

My bull is white like the silver fish in the river
white like the shimmering crane bird on the river bank
white like fresh milk!
His roar is like the thunder to the Turkish cannon on the steep shore.
My bull is dark like the raincloud in the storm.
He is like summer and winter.
Half of him is dark like the storm cloud,
half of him is light like sunshine.
His back shines like the morning star.
His forehead is like a flag, calling people from a distance,
he resembles the rainbow.

I will water him at the river,
with my spear I shall drive my enemies.
Let them water their herds at the well;
the river belongs to me and my bull.
Drink, my bull, from the river; I am here
to guard you with my spear.

Dinka tribe

Close to Nature

The sun shines through a mist,
a golden ball through the fresh dew
when men in the sunset
in worlds of marble and steel
prepare to sleep.

On warm bamboo beds we lie
awaken with the fresh morning
and learn to balance earthenware
vessels on our trained heads
as we head to streams
where naked children bathe and play.

In tranquility and calm, we hurry not
looking up at the elements
to tell the time of day,
while men beyond speed away at jet
speed to meet loads of duties.

Close to nature, our minds
remain impressionable, like the soft
sandy earth around our round huts;
engraved on them are footprints
of the child and the lamb
and the little carefree chicks.

We learn from nature
and grow at the steady and sure pace
of the stately iroko tree
and watch our dark reflections
on pristine springs of rocky coolness.

        Nnamdi Ben Nneji

Inside my Zulu Hut

It is a hive
without any bees
to build the walls
with golden bricks of honey.
A cave cluttered
with a millstone,
calabashes of sour milk
claypots of foaming beer
sleeping grass mats

wooden head rests
tanned goat skins
tied with riempies
to wattle rafters
blackened by the smoke
of kneaded cow dung
burning under
the three-legged pot
on the earthen floor
to cook my porridge.

  Oswald Mbuyiseni Mtshali

I Tell the Bees

He left for good in the early hours with just
one book, held tight in his left hand:
The Cyclopedia of Everything Pertaining
to the Care of the Honey-Bee; Bees, Hives,
Honey, Implements, Honey-Plants, Etc.
And I begrudged him every single et cetera,
every honey-strainer and cucumber blossom,
every bee-wing and flown year and dead eye,
I went outside when the sun rose, whistling
to call them out as I walked towards the hive.
I pressed my cheek against the wood, opened
my synapses to bee hum, I could smell bee hum.
'It's over, honies,' I whispered, 'and now you're mine.'

            Jo Shapcott

Gathering the Honey

Whenever you would unseal their noble home, and the honey
they keep in store, first bathe the entrance, moistening it
with a draught of water, and follow it with smoke held out
in your hand. Their anger knows no bounds, and when hurt
they suck venom into their stings, and leave their hidden lances
fixed in a vein, laying down their lives in the wound they make.
Twice men gather the rich produce: there are two seasons
for harvest, as soon as Taygete the Pleiad has shown
her lovely face to Earth and spurned the Ocean stream
with scornful foot, and when that same star fleeing watery Pisces
sinks more sadly from the sky into the wintry waves.
But if you fear a harsh winter, and would spare their future,
and pity their bruised spirits, and shattered fortunes,
who would then hesitate to fumigate them with thyme
and cut away the empty wax? For often a newt has nibbled
the combs unseen, cockroaches, light-averse, fill the cells,
and the useless drone sits down to another's food:
or the fierce hornet has attacked with unequal weapons,
or the dread race of moths, or the spider, hated by Minerva,
hangs her loose webs in the entrances.
The more is taken, the more eagerly they devote themselves
to repairing the damage to their troubled species,
and filling the cells, and building their stores from flowers.

Virgil
from *The Georgics* Book IV,
translated by A. S. Kline

DESTRUCTION

SO EDEN SANK TO GRIEF

Illustration by Holly Phoa year 10

Nothing Gold can Stay

Nature's first green is gold,
Her hardest hue to hold.
Her early leaf's a flower;
But only so an hour.
Then leaf subsides to leaf.
So Eden sank to grief,
So dawn goes down to day.
Nothing gold can stay.

                Robert Frost

'Report to Wordsworth'

You should be here, Nature has need of you.
She has been laid waste. Smothered by the smog,
the flowers are mute, and the birds are few
in a sky slowing like a dying clock.
All hopes of Proteus rising from the sea
have sunk; he is entombed in the waste
we dump. Triton's notes struggle to be free,
his famous horns are choked, his eyes are dazed,
and Neptune lies helpless as beached as a whale,
while insatiate man moves in for the kill.
Poetry and piety have begun to fail,
as Nature's mighty heart is lying still.
O see the widening in the sky,
God is labouring to utter his last cry.

                                    Boey Kim Cheng

Lily of the Valley

A white-faced hanging-her-head
well-rooted woman used to live here.
Under the hips of the hills
in the arms of the valley.

Day after night after day
she stood here.
Hanging her head and letting fall her glances
on the tilted surface of the river.

Which was in fact the exact diameter
of the sphere of the valley.
The very tip of the cone
down which heaven was endlessly trickling.

And trees leaves stars everything
was always running down through stones
to this lowest level
of the lull between earth waves.

And hanging her head she said
I'm not leaving this valley
I'm going to bury my feet in the earth
they'll never shift me.

But they did.

                    Alice Oswald

Trailing Arbutus

Like a virgin whose beauty
Can tease and entice,
So was the arbutus,
Forbidden but nice.

She trailed her long vines
Emitting her scent
But permission to pick her,
Not given consent.

Endangered, her species,
Protected by law,
To the plight of this flower,
My sight had a flaw.

Embracing her beauty,
I held her up close
And drank in her fragrance
That outranked the rose.

As guilt ran all through me,
For her roots now exposed;
With regret, I now threw her;
This flower disposed.

I watched as she wilted,
My conscious, it pricked,
I watched her lie dying;
Guilty, the verdict.

Trailing arbutus,
Remembered so well;
No more have I seen her
Or fragrance to smell.

       Gloria Sarasin

Endangered Species

No wonder we love the whales. Do they not carry
Our warm blood below and we remember
Falling asleep in a feeling element
And our voices beating a musical way

To a larger kindred, around the world? Mostly
We wake too quickly, the sleep runs off our heads
And we are employed at once in the usual
Coveting and schemes. I was luckier today

And remembered leaving a house in the Dales
Like home for a night, the four under one roof,
I left them sleeping without a moon *or* stars
And followed my dreaming self along a road.

Daylight augmented in a fine rain.
I had the sensation of drawing on my face.
But for the animals (and they had gathered
The dark standing in fields and now appeared

Replete) the night dissolved, but in the light,
A grey-eyed light, under the draining hills
Some pools of woodland remained and in them owls
And beside my sleepwalking, along the borders

Owls accompanied me, they were echoing
From wood to wood, into the hesitant day
I carried the owls in their surviving wells
Of night-time. The fittest are a fatal breed.

They'd do without sleep if they possibly could
And meter it for the rest of us. I like
Humans who harbour the dark in their open
Eyes all day. They seem more kin, more kind. They are

The ones not listening while the ruling voices
Further impair our hearing. They are away
With the owls, they ride the dreaming hooting hills
Down, down, into an infinite pacific.

                                    David Constantine

The Flower-Fed Buffaloes

The flower-fed buffaloes of the spring
In the days of long ago,
Ranged where the locomotives sing
And the prairie flowers lie low;
The tossing, blooming, perfumed grass
Is swept away by wheat,
Wheels and wheels and wheels spin by
In the spring that still is sweet.
But the flower-fed buffaloes of the spring
Left us long ago.
They gore no more, they bellow no more,
They trundle around the hills no more:
With the Blackfeet lying low,
With the Pawnees lying low.

                    Vachel Lindsay

Pheasant

You said you would kill it this morning.
Do not kill it. It startles me still,
The jut of that odd, dark head, pacing

Through the uncut grass on the elm's hill.
It is something to own a pheasant,
Or just to be visited at all.

I am not mystical: it isn't
As if I thought it had a spirit.
It is simply in its element.

That gives it a kingliness, a right.
The print of its big foot last winter,
The trail-track, on the snow in our court

The wonder of it, in that pallor,
Through crosshatch of sparrow and starling.
Is it its rareness, then? It is rare.

But a dozen would be worth having,
A hundred, on that hill — green and red,
Crossing and recrossing: a fine thing!

It is such a good shape, so vivid.
It's a little cornucopia.
It unclaps, brown as a leaf, and loud,

Settles in the elm, and is easy.
It was sunning in the narcissi.
I trespass stupidly. Let be, let be.

       Sylvia Plath

Almanac

The indifferent rivers
Will keep on flowing to the sea
Or ruinously overflowing dikes,
Ancient handiwork of determined men.
The glaciers will continue to grate,
Smoothing what lies beneath them.
Or suddenly fall headlong,
Cutting short fir trees' lives.
The sea, captive between
Two continents, will go on struggling,
Always miserly with its riches.
Sun, stars, planets and comets
Will continue on their course.
Earth too will fear the immutable
Laws of the universe.
Not us. We, rebellious offspring
With great brainpower, little sense,
Will destroy, defile,
Always more feverishly.
Very soon we will extend the desert
Into the Amazon forests,
Into the living heart of our cities,
Into our very hearts.

       Primo Levi

Estuary

RUSH	SEDGE	COUCH	MARRAM	BENT
CURLEW	WHIMBREL	GULL	LAPWING	TERN
ESSO	MOBIL	BP	EXXON	SHELL

                                              Ian Hamilton Finlay

Harvest Hymn

We spray the fields and scatter
The poison on the ground
So that no wicked wild flowers
Upon our farm be found.
We like whatever helps us
To line our purse with pence;
The twenty-four-hour broiler-house
And neat electric fence.
All concrete sheds around us
And Jaguars in the yard,
The telly lounge and deep-freeze
Are ours from working hard.
We fire the fields for harvest,
The hedges swell the flame,
The oak trees and the cottages
From which our fathers came.
We give no compensation,
The earth is ours today,
And if we lose on arable,
The bungalows will pay.
All concrete sheds . . . etc.

                John Betjeman

The Recital of Lost Cities

It started with the polar ice caps.
A slight increase in temperature and the quiet
was shattered. The Australian Antarctic
wandered all over the Norwegian Dependency
as mountainous fragments lurched free
with a groan like ship's mahogany.

And then there was the continental shift:
everywhere you went, America was coming closer.
Hot weather brought plague and revolution.
Nations disappeared or renamed themselves
as borders moved, in, out, in, out,
with tidal persistence and threat.

Cartographers dealt in picture postcards.
The printing plates for the last atlas
were archived unused. Their irrelevant contours
gathered dust, locked in a vault
to save the public from the past
and the danger of wrong directions.

The sea rose by inches, unravelled the coastline,
eased across the lowlands and licked at the hills
where people gathered to remember names:
Calcutta, Tokyo, San Francisco,
Venice, Amsterdam, Baku,
Alexandria, Santo Domingo . . .

                Lavinia Greenlaw

The Woman in the Moon

Darlings, I write to you from the moon
where I hide behind famous light.
How could you think it was ever a man up here?
A cow jumped over. The dish ran away with the spoon.

What reached me here were your prayers, griefs,
here's the craic, losses and longings, your lives
so brief, mine long, long, a talented loneliness.
I must have a thousand names for the earth, my blue vocation.

Round I go, the moon a diet of light, sliver of pear,
wedge of lemon, slice of melon, half an orange, onion;
your human music falling like petals through space,
the childbirth song, the lover's song, the song of death.

Devoted as words to things, I stare and stare;
deserts where forests were, vanishing seas. When your night comes,
I see you staring back as though you can hear my *Darlings,
what have you done, what have you done to the earth?*

                                        Carol Ann Duffy

SUSTAINABILITY

BEGIN AFRESH AFRESH AFRESH

Illustration by Camilla Snell year 13

The Trees

The trees are coming into leaf
Like something almost being said;
The recent buds relax and spread,
Their greenness is a kind of grief.

Is it that they are born again
And we grow old? No, they die too,
Their yearly trick of looking new
Is written down in rings of grain.

Yet still the unresting castles thresh
In fullgrown thickness every May.
Last year is dead, they seem to say,
Begin afresh, afresh, afresh.

                    Philip Larkin

The Eclipse

I stood out in the open cold
To see the essence of the eclipse
Which was its perfect darkness.

I stood in the cold on the porch
And could not think of anything so perfect
As man's hope of light in the face of darkness.

                      Richard Eberhart

The Cloud (excerpts from ...)

I bring fresh showers for the thirsting flowers,
    From the seas and the streams;
I bear light shade for the leaves when laid
    In their noonday dreams.
From my wings are shaken the dews that waken
    The sweet buds every one,
When rocked to rest on their mother's breast,
    As she dances about the sun.
I wield the flail of the lashing hail,
    And whiten the green plains under,
And then again I dissolve it in rain,
    And laugh as I pass in thunder.

I sift the snow on the mountains below,
    And their great pines groan aghast;
And all the night 'tis my pillow white,
    While I sleep in the arms of the blast.
Sublime on the towers of my skiey bowers,
    Lightning my pilot sits,
In a cavern under is fretted the thunder,
    It struggles and howls at fits;
Over earth and ocean, with gentle motion,
    This pilot is guiding me,
Lured by the love of the genii that move
    In the depths of the purple sea;
Over the rills, and the crags, and the hills,
    Over the lakes and the plains,

Wherever he dream, under mountain or stream
   The Spirit he loves remains;
And I all the while bask in heaven's blue smile,
   Whilst he is dissolving in rains.

I am the daughter of earth and water,
   And the nursling of the sky;
I pass through the pores of the ocean and shores;
   I change, but I cannot die.
For after the rain when with never a stain,
   The pavilion of heaven is bare,
And the winds and sunbeams with their convex gleams,
   Build up the blue dome of air,
I silently laugh at my own cenotaph,
   And out of the caverns of rain,
Like a child from the womb, like a ghost from the tomb,
   I arise and unbuild it again.

                              Percy Bysshe Shelley

Si Dieu N'existait Pas

No one invents an absence:
Cadmium yellow, duckweed, the capercaillie
— see how the hand we would name restrains itself
till all our stories end in monochrome;

the path through the meadow
reaching no logical end;
nothing but colour: bedstraw and ladies' mantle;
nothing sequential; nothing as chapter and verse.

No one invents the quiet that runs in the grass,
the summer wind, the sky, the meadowlark;
and always the gift of the world, the undecided:
first light and damson blue ad infinitum.

                              John Burnside

Heavenly Grass

My feet took a walk in heavenly grass.
All day while the sky shone clear as glass.
My feet took a walk in heavenly grass,
All night while the lonesome stars rolled past.
Then my feet come down to walk on earth,
And my mother cried when she give me birth.
Now my feet walk far and my feet walk fast,
But they still got an itch for heavenly grass.
But they still got an itch for heavenly grass.

                        Tennessee Williams

Untitled – (Tomorrow's Child)

Without a name; an unseen face
and knowing not your time nor place
Tomorrow's Child, though yet unborn,
I met you first last Tuesday morn.

A wise friend introduced us two,
and through his sobering point of view
I saw a day that you would see;
a day for you, but not for me

Knowing you has changed my thinking,
for I never had an inkling
that perhaps the things I do
might someday, somehow, threaten you

Tomorrow's Child, my daughter-son
I'm afraid I've just begun
to think of you and of your good,
though always having known I should.

Begin I will to weigh the cost
of what I squander; what is lost
if ever I forget that you
will someday come to live here too.

                      Glenn Thomas

I'm Alive, I Believe In Everything

Self. Brotherhood. God. Zeus. Communism.
Capitalism. Buddha. Vinyl records.
Baseball. Ink. Trees. Cures for disease.
Saltwater. Literature. Walking. Waking.
Arguments. Decisions. Ambiguity. Absolutes.
Presence. Absence. Positive and Negative.
Empathy. Apathy. Sympathy and entropy.
Verbs are necessary. So are nouns.
Empty skies. Dark vacuums of night.
Visions. Revisions. Innocence.
I've seen All the empty spaces yet to be filled.
I've heard All of the sounds that will collect
at the end of the world.
And the silence that follows.

I'm alive, I believe in everything
I'm alive, I believe in it all.

Waves lapping on the shore.
Skies on fire at sunset.
Old men dancing on the streets.
Paradox and possibility.
Sense and sensibility.
Cold logic and half truth.
Final steps and first impressions.
Fools and fine intelligence.
Chaos and clean horizons.

Vague notions and concrete certainty.
Optimism in the face of adversity.

I'm alive, I believe in everything
I'm alive, I believe in it all.

                Lesley Choyce

A Light Exists in Spring

A Light exists in Spring
Not present on the Year
At any other period—
When March is scarcely here

A Color stands abroad
On Solitary Fields
That Science cannot overtake
But Human Nature feels.

It waits upon the Lawn,
It shows the furthest Tree
Upon the furthest Slope you know
It almost speaks to you.

Then as Horizons step
Or Noons report away
Without the Formula of sound
It passes and we stay—

A quality of loss
Affecting our Content
As Trade had suddenly encroached
Upon a Sacrament.

     Emily Dickinson

Illustration by Sarah Geake year 13

Monkton School and the Anthologise Competition

In the past, Monkton Senior School Library and Art departments have worked closely with Bath Festivals, who brought the competition to our attention in December 2011. They gave supportive training to both teachers, encouraging a collaborative approach and enabling a supportive role towards the students to release their creativity.

All involved were immediately enthusiastic, largely due to the passion for poetry shared by both the Librarian, Mrs Webb, and Art teacher Mrs Hildreth, who had already been instrumental in setting up a 'Pass on a Poem' group at school, which is open to members of the school and local residents. ('Pass on a Poem' has been part of Bath culture for the past eight years, it is an organisation started by Francis Stadlen for the pleasure of listening to favourite poems read out loud to groups ranging from two or three members to fifty or sixty, and now has bases all around the country. The school embraced its own group last year based at the library.)

The theme of nature and environment, described as ecological poetry, was chosen as it reflects the school's desire for a sustainable future, one that the school as a whole are working towards. We are hoping to gain our Green Flag status in the near future.

The group of seven pupils who took part was chosen largely due their love of books and art and our personal knowledge of whether they would be able to commit to such a project. They ranged across all year groups from years nine to thirteen. The group became cohesive very quickly and worked very well as a team. This created a lovely forum for them to work creatively, discussing many diverse ways of approaching their topic.

Both Mrs Hildreth and Mrs Webb agree that nurturing the enjoyment and love of poetry can often be overlooked in schools because of academic pressures, and the competition was an excellent way to continue to encourage a better love of its beauty and poignancy. The group all agreed that it was immensely enjoyable. The project was done out of class time, the group giving up their own time to put the anthology together, reflecting a high level of commitment. The encouragement that they were given to look at creative ways to design chapters resulted in a book whose first chapter, 'Appreciation of Nature', naturally progressed through 'Destruction' to 'Sustainability'. All poems were chosen by the pupils and included a wide range of classical, contemporary and multicultural works.

Once the poems were selected, the year thirteen art students' work was chosen, in consultation with them, to sit alongside some of the beautiful poetry the team had chosen. The use of poetry in art is deeply encouraged and forms the basis of much of the artwork produced by an exceptionally successful department.

The day the group went to the Flagship school to present their work to Carol Ann Duffy was enjoyed immensely by all. The students loved the event, especially listening to Carol Ann reading her own work accompanied by John Sampson's brilliant musical pipes.

Monkton's vision for the development of all pupils can be summed up in four words, confidence, integrity, sensitivity and ambition, all of which were demonstrated by this group during the project.

Monkton Senior School is the senior school of Monkton Combe School, based on the outskirts of Bath. It is a boarding school with over seven hundred pupils combined with its prep and pre-prep. Both Prep and Senior School are boarding and day schools.

Acknowledgements

Thanks must go to Jane Hildreth for the design of the competition entry, Jane Hildreth and Lynne Webb for the coordination and compilation of the anthology and the following pupils for poetry and art work:

Robert Warwood-Hart year 9
Jonathan Hambly year 10
Sian Cogan year 10
Holly Phoa year 10
Daniel Mangles year 10
Olivia Wameyo year 12
Sarah Pritchard year 13
Sarah Geake year 13
Christina Lee year 13
Ziv Wu year 13
Kate Slade year 13
Camilla Snell year 13
Nicola Murray year 13

Permission acknowledgements

John Betjeman, 'Harvest Hymn', from *Collected Poems*, by John Betjeman © 1955, 1958, 1962, 1964, 1968, 1970, 1979, 1981, 1982, 2001. Reproduced by permission of John Murray (Publishers). Jean Binta Breeze, 'Earth Cries', from *The Arrival of Brighteyes and Other Poems* (Bloodaxe Books, 2000). Lesley Choyce, 'I'm Alive, I Believe in Everything' from *Beautiful Sadness* (1998), by kind permission of Lesley Choyce. There is a Youtube video of it and a spoken word recording version at www.lesleychoyce.com. David Constantine, 'Endangered Species', from *Collected Poems* (Bloodaxe Books, 2004). Carol Ann Duffy, 'The Woman in the Moon', from *Granta* 108 (Autumn 2008), by kind permission of Carol Ann Duffy. Richard Eberhart, 'The Eclipse', from *Collected Poems 1930–1986*, permission for reproduction granted by the Richard Eberhart Estate. Lavinia Greenlaw, 'The Recital of Lost Cities', from *Night Photograph* (1993), by kind permission of Faber and Faber Ltd. Seamus Heaney, 'Death of a Naturalist' from *Death of a Naturalist* (1966), by kind permission of Faber and Faber Ltd. Langston Hughes, 'The Negro Speaks of Rivers' from *The Collected Poems of Langston Hughes*; ed. Arnold Rampersad (1995), by kind permission of Alfred A. Knopf Inc. Ted Hughes, 'The River in March' from *Season Songs* (1976), by kind permission of Faber and Faber Ltd. Kathleen Jamie, 'The Case' from *The Hand That Sees*, ed. by Stewart Conn (2000), by kind permission of Kathleen Jamie. Philip Larkin, 'The Trees', from *Collected Poems* (1988), by kind permission of Faber and Faber Ltd. Primo Levi, 'Almanac', from *Collected Poems* (1988), by kind permission of Faber and Faber Ltd. W. S. Merwin, 'Place', from *Selected Poems* (Bloodaxe Books, 2007). Oswald Mbuyiseni Mtshali, 'Inside my Zulu Hut', from *Sounds of a Cowhide Drum*, Oswald Mbuyiseni Mtshali, Jacana Media,

2012 (originally published 1971). Riad Nourallah, 'An Alphabet for the Planet', by kind permission of Riad Nourallah. Alice Oswald, 'Lily of the Valley', from *Weeds and Wild Flowers* (2009), by kind permission of Faber and Faber Ltd. Sylvia Plath, 'Pheasant', from *Collected Poems* (1981), by kind permission of Faber and Faber Ltd. Theodore Roethke, 'Moss-Gathering', from *Collected Poems* (1968), by kind permission of Faber and Faber Ltd. Gloria Sarasin, 'Trailing Arbutus', by kind permission of Gloria L. Sarasin. Susan Taylor, 'Cultivators', from *Lincoln Green* (1977), by kind permission of Susan Taylor. Virgil, 'Gathering the Honey', from *The Georgics* Bk IV trans. A. S. Kline, by kind permission of A. S. Kline. Tennessee Williams, 'Heavenly Grass', from *The Collected Poems of Tennessee Williams* by Tennessee Williams. Copyright © 1937 by The University of The South. Reprinted by permission of Georges Borchardt, Inc. for the Estate of Tennessee Williams. All rights reserved. Benjamin Zephaniah, 'A Beetle Called Derek', from *Talking Turkeys* (London, 1994), copyright © Benjamin Zephaniah 1994.